IMAGINARY BORDERS

XIUHTEZCATL MARTINEZ
WITH CONTRIBUTIONS BY RUSSELL MENDELL

PENGUIN WORKSHOP

To mi hermanita Tonantzin, for the light you carry that inspires us to keep fighting—XM

PENGUIN WORKSHOP
An Imprint of Penguin Random House LLC, New York

The publisher does not have any control over and does not assume any responsibility for author or third-party websites or their content.

Text copyright © 2020 by Xiuhtezcatl Martinez. Illustrations copyright © 2020 by Penguin Random House LLC. All rights reserved. Published by Penguin Workshop, an imprint of Penguin Random House LLC, New York. PENGUIN and PENGUIN WORKSHOP are trademarks of Penguin Books Ltd, and the W colophon is a registered trademark of Penguin Random House LLC. Manufactured in China.

Visit us online at www.penguinrandomhouse.com.

Library of Congress Cataloging-in-Publication Data is available upon request.

ISBN 9780593094136   10 9 8 7 6 5 4 3 2 1

PROLOGUE

When adults make blatant generalizations about our generation, our disinterest in politics, and our disengagement from the real world, they're not seeing the whole picture. They don't see that the older generations who've shaped our society have done a really shitty job of creating a world that we feel inspired to engage with. We're not passive because we're ignorant and don't understand the challenges our world faces. We get that the changing climate is threatening our future. We can see the corruption of big-industry money in politics. We see the injustice and hatred: from unchecked police brutality, to families being separated at the US-Mexico border, to militarized police using extreme force against Water Protectors at Standing Rock. It is literally being live-streamed and documented in a way that has never been seen before.

Our generation has the tools to understand what's going on better than any before us, through social media and technology. But we often remain silent because these stories of crisis are never met with stories of solution. It's hard to find hope in the ocean of negative, depressing, fear-based media. So a lot of us check out. To cope with the broken world we live in, we distract ourselves with social media, drugs, partying, and an endless black hole of viral dance videos, leaned-out trap rappers, and Fortnite memes.

I've been involved in the climate movement since I was six years old: standing to protect sacred land from pipelines, suing the US federal government for knowingly contributing to the climate crisis, demanding binding policy change and a Just Transition from fossil fuels, and eventually becoming the Youth Director of the global organization Earth Guardians. Equally important to my climate activism has been my journey to deconstruct the broken story around our future and reinvent what our collective movement can look like. We are the most diverse and most connected generation in history. We need the story of our movements to reflect that, so we can better understand the power we have to shape our world in the face of the crisis at hand.

We all have a responsibility to be a part of this redefinition of movement culture. It's time to reclaim our space in these movements. Until every Friday night is an after-party for the FridaysForFuture school walkout y'all did earlier that day. Till our movements speak a language of culture and power, drippin' in art, color, and diversity. Till fighting for what we believe in is something that becomes a part of us, not an external cause or use of energy.

This book isn't about changing the world—it's about building it together. Whether the content of these pages helps you find it or not, you have a part to play. Because the future is as much yours as it is mine. And that's a beautiful thing.

IMAGINARY BORDERS

From "Boombox Warfare" (featuring Jaden Smith):

> *I can feel the sound*
> *I can feel the sound*
> *We on a wave*
> *We on a wave now . . .*

Even if you don't have a driver's license, I'd say that most people know that driving in LA can suuuck. Luckily, I left my meeting just in time to beat the 5:00 p.m. traffic on my way to San Diego. As I was leaving, I turned on a podcast that was recommended to me by a student I had met at a college speaking gig a few days before. The podcast was called *The Joe Rogan Experience*. In this particular episode, comedian Joe Rogan was in conversation with David Wallace-Wells, a journalist and author of *The Uninhabitable Earth*, which, as you can probably imagine, is about the end of the world.

Wells's end of the world didn't have to do with the Sun swallowing Earth, an alien invasion, or super-fast zombies. It had to do with something much more real. In case you haven't heard, human beings are warming the planet. The burning of fossil fuels has caused the atmosphere to fill with greenhouse gases, which trap heat. Since the Industrial Revolution, heat-trapping gases like carbon dioxide (CO_2) have risen by nearly 50 percent because of us. More than half of that CO_2 is just from the last thirty years. All the extra greenhouse gases have led to an increase in global temperatures of 1.1 degree Celsius.

That may not sound like a lot, but it has caused the last five years to be the hottest in recorded history. Rising temperatures have led to more frequent and extreme heat waves, floods, droughts, and hurricanes, because a warmer world also means a wetter one (hence the flooding and storms). In 2018, extreme-weather events, proven to be worsened by climate change, cost taxpayers $91 billion in cleanup, prevention, and restoration in the United States. That doesn't even count the human cost, as hundreds lost their lives to these natural disasters.

When we think of the climate crisis, we picture

classic images of ice caps melting, sea levels rising, and polar bears drowning. But more than isolated weather events, you're about to see that the climate crisis is more like a fucked-up web that connects and impacts every single thing we care about. It amplifies all the existing problems we experience today, from racial injustice to economic inequality to health issues to food access to war. It affects our economies, our politics, and our cultures.

"So how much trouble are we in, legitimately?" Rogan asked.

"I mean, it's pretty bad already, and it's going to get, I think, a lot, lot worse," Wallace-Wells replied. As I merged onto the highway, Wallace-Wells began to speak in a way that made me feel the urgency and proximity of our climate crisis. The first thing he brought up was the wildfires that ripped through California in 2018. "Last year, there were flames hopping over the 405," Wallace-Wells said. That visual created a flashback to seeing my homies posting videos all over Instagram when the fires hit LA. It looked like some Mordor, end-of-the-world,

Hollywood shit. And there I was, only four months later, just a few dozen miles south of where the hillside had been swallowed by fire, now under a clear blue sky. Everything seemed fine. Like, beyond fine. Nature was poppin' off. The hills were glowing with all kinds of flowers that had just bloomed, and there were hundreds of butterflies lazily floating through the air all around me, making their way north in a mass migration from Mexico. It was beautiful.

Even though I was safe in that moment, it didn't make any of what Wallace-Wells was explaining less true or less terrifying. He went on about the fires: "There're scientific estimates that say that, by the end of the century, they will get sixty-four times worse. . . . [That] would mean more than half of California burning every year." Wallace-Wells then went on to say that climate damages would create about $600 trillion in expenses by the end of the century. To put that in perspective, that's twice as much as all the wealth in the world today. I caught myself laughing, thinking about all the people who say acting on climate is too expensive. Homie was telling me that on our current trajectory, we are moving toward two degrees Celsius of warming, which the UN calls a "point of disaster" and island nations are referring to as "climate genocide." By the time we reach that two-degree Celsius (3.6 degrees Fahrenheit) increase, we'll likely experience the death of almost all coral reefs on the planet, entire polar ice sheets melting in the summer, and about five meters (sixteen feet) of sea-level rise. To top it off, we're barreling closer toward a runaway climate scenario that could send us to a three-, four-, or even five-degree Celsius temperature rise. And, apparently, a two-degree increase is our best-case scenario.

That's the fuckedest best-case scenario I've ever heard.

Joe Rogan and I were both shook. This moment brought back memories of how it all started for me, at age six when I asked my mom how people can live their lives every day, go to school and go to work without thinking about this. *This* being that humans are causing the greatest environmental catastrophes on Earth. Wallace-Wells spoke about how even for someone like him, who has read thousands of scientific papers on the topic and understands the urgency of the climate crisis, part of him still doesn't want to admit the reality of the world we have created. For those of us privileged enough to not be directly faced with the crisis on a daily basis, our instinct is to turn away and to leave the problem to the UN, world leaders, and activists. We do everything in our power to keep this story as far from our world as we possibly can. When we deny our roles and ignore the imminent danger that is already affecting our planet, we relinquish our responsibility to change anything about the way we're living.

I let it all wash over me. Even after thirteen years of speaking, writing, and thinking about this issue, it never felt quite this big. I felt angry and overwhelmed. But even as the podcast wrapped up, it failed to address what I see as the most critical piece of this conversation: the deep need to create a cultural shift that includes people in every facet of society.

It's not going to be good enough to just pull all the CO_2 out of the atmosphere with a magic technology that allows us to continue course. It's not good enough to keep taking resources from the planet via a different renewable energy source. The challenges we face are bigger than just energy, carbon emissions, or extreme-weather events. All that we're up against—our changing climate, fossil-fuel extraction, industrial agriculture—is deeply connected. At the root of all these issues lies a fundamental loss of the piece of our humanity that allows us to see ourselves as a part of a larger system.

Not only have we lost our connection to the earth, but humans have created societies based on the exploitation of the very resources that support our existence. Our dissociation from the natural world has led to the system of self-destruction we see today. We are cutting out critical pieces of this deeply interdependent web of life, and unless we flip a super-tight one-eighty, it's just a matter of a few years before the entire web unravels.

The truth is, what we do in the next ten years will affect the following thousands of years of life on Earth. And yet we're not doing enough, many are doing nothing, and some still think climate change is not an issue. It's become ridiculously clear that if we want to address the climate crisis, we must completely redesign the narrative around it. Everything from how we think about this issue to how we talk about this issue to how we react to this issue needs to change. We're at a tipping point that requires every conversation around this crisis to result in direct action. We have an opportunity to spread a narrative that invites and inspires solutions—one that is different than what we've seen before.

As I checked into my room and dropped my bags, all of these thoughts were racing through my head. I did what I usually do when there's more on my mind than I can process: I started to write lyrics. It was like meditation to me. Moments like these—when I feel completely lost, unsure of my path and my purpose; when I feel depressed about the world and unable to talk to anyone about it—I write.

Over the past few years, music has completely redefined my relationship to my voice and to this movement. Music has helped me reclaim my story—

both as an activist and as an artist. Seeing thousands of people turning up with us, listening to songs written about our movements, I realized that this is what revolution looks like. We need to use our art and expression to build power and shape our movements.

We can no longer bind the climate movement to a linear idea of political action and traditional activism. Change has to address the deeper societal injustices facing the most vulnerable of our communities. Change has to come from every vertical of our society—from the clubs and house parties we're getting lit at, to the businesses we start, to the way we pursue education, to what we put on our plate and on the Gram. This is bigger and more critical than being an activist. This is recognizing the piece of our humanity that gives us the authority and power to use every action and every step we take to create change. We must infuse the lives we already live as athletes, artists, students, rebels, and dreamers with actions that reflect the power we all have.

It's about all of us. It's about you.

You see this rhythm speaks
Study the history
People singing songs of freedom while we
*   marching in the street . . .*

Even though I was born in Boulder, Colorado, part of me has always felt deeply connected to where my roots lie in Mexico. I grew up with the teaching that a home is so much more than a building or a city. For my people, the Mexica people, our connection to place is founded in a deep and sacred respect for the soil we built our cities on. After hundreds of years of searching, my ancestors found their home in Mexico Tenochtitlán (modern-day Mexico City). They built a thriving metropolis that coexisted with the natural paradise that was already there. In our teachings, in our ceremonies, in our philosophies, and in our science, we saw ourselves simply as pieces within a larger story of creation—

not separate from the elements that gave us life. These teachings were at the foundation of my perception of self and of the world. Hundreds of years after Spain colonized our home and exploited our sacred land, our culture survived because families like mine carried it on and protected it for future generations.

I grew up visiting my dad's family's home in Santa Cruz Acalpixca, a small town in the hills of Xochimilco, Mexico City. It was there that I was offered a window into the world he grew up in. The stories he told me about the beauty, abundance, and magic in a simpler life inspired me. Everything my family taught me about our culture and the strong lineage of warriors, scholars, and artists we came from anchored me deeper in Mexico. It connected me to the ceremonial sites that survived colonization, where my family practiced our holy traditions.

After everything my people and so many indigenous nations have endured as a result of centuries of oppression and genocide, discrimination and exploitation, we're also among the people most threatened by our climate crisis.

Like other marginalized communities, our vulnerability to climate change is about more than just geographic placement. Our susceptibility to the dire impacts of a changing climate is heightened by many systems of oppression that have harmed our communities for generations. People of color are being disproportionately hit by warming-driven disasters. Systemic injustices of economic disparity and discriminatory city planning push communities of color to the greatest danger zones for flooding and superstorms. In 2005, Hurricane Katrina devastated New Orleans, killing close to eighteen hundred people. The worst impacts were felt in New Orleans' Lower Ninth Ward, a majority black neighborhood where the average resident was living on an income of under $20,000 a year. This disaster is one of many examples of marginalized communities being driven to the front lines of the climate crisis.

In Mexico, the damages from climate change are vast and growing worse every year. The expansion and exploitation of Mexico City has led to severe imbalances for a growing metropolitan area of twenty-two million people. The population and demand for water are increasing in tandem with warming and drought. Upward of 20 percent of people in Mexico City don't have access to running water every day. My family in Xochimilco is among that group. Once or twice a week, they fill up huge blue buckets with water for washing their clothes, dishes, flushing the toilet, and showering. Although my family lives in what most people in the States would perceive as poverty, they are mad fortunate compared to many of our friends in surrounding neighborhoods.

I've read stories of families not far from my family's home in Acalpixca that are spending 10 percent of their income on water brought by truck or by donkey. The average person in an affluent part of Mexico City uses ten times as much water as these poor families and pays one tenth of the cost. This inequality is only going to get worse as drought and water scarcity increases and as the city continues to exhaust its underground aquifers. Families like mine who are already experiencing water shortages are also disproportionately impacted by a changing climate and an unjust distribution of resources and infrastructure.

If we widen the scope even further, climate change is an issue that reaches beyond city limits and across borders. Studies out of Colorado University have linked migration from Mexico to drought and extreme-weather events. As Mexican farmers' land dries up, they're more likely to come north for shelter and work. One study predicts that 10 percent of Mexicans ages fifteen to sixty-five could move north because of the climate crisis. The result could potentially displace millions of people and magnify existing political tensions over immigration. The same is true for other countries in Central America where extended drought is forcing people from their homes. The irony is that the nations discriminating against immigrants are the ones responsible for releasing the most carbon dioxide into the atmosphere, which is creating the conditions that are causing more people to seek refuge. For instance, the average American emits more than four times the amount of carbon as the average Mexican and roughly sixteen times more than the average person from Guatemala, Honduras, or El Salvador.

Climate change and immigration are two things that have been at the forefront of my life since I was a little kid, and it's never been clearer how connected the two are. So when the media was flooded by talk of migrant caravans and President Trump declaring the US-Mexico border a national emergency, it brought up a lot for me. Seeing the images and reading the stories of children held in cages, separated from their families, left me absolutely crushed. It made me think of every person I loved who has crossed that border to be with their family, struggled to send money back home, or searched for opportunities for a better life. I saw my little cousins, nieces, and nephews in the faces of the kids being taken from their parents. This complete lack of humanity driven by the US government is the real crisis, not the influx of families coming north.

This kind of inhumanity is only a preview of what's to come if we don't address the realities we're up against. Experts believe that climate change will create an additional two hundred million refugees in the next thirty years, and high-end estimates are predicting a billion people displaced by the end of the century. These changes are going to seriously affect our society as a whole, and it will become impossible to ignore the connection between a warming atmosphere and racial oppression.

This intricate web of impacts from the crisis is so much vaster than most people can imagine. Beyond migration, it is also leading to an increase in violence and war. The cascading effects of climate change contribute to food and resource shortage, leading to poverty and scarcity, which results in increased conflict around the world. It's estimated that for each half degree in temperature rise, there will be 10 to 20 percent more war globally.

Take, for instance, the Syrian refugee crisis. Scientists found that the worst drought in that region's history was partially responsible for the bloody civil war that has led to millions of refugees seeking asylum in surrounding countries, Europe, and the United States. The loss of crops due to the drought caused food prices to rise, which exacerbated poverty and desperation and became a precursor to the instability and violence.

Like in the United States, Europe has seen an increase in people seeking refuge from climate-related conflict, which has led to a rise in racism and xenophobia. This anti-immigrant sentiment contributed to the Brexit vote in the United Kingdom and the rise of nationalistic right-wing parties in many countries throughout Europe. Half of the greenhouse gases are being emitted by Europe and North America, but the people experiencing the worst impacts of climate change are in the Middle East, Africa, Latin America, Southern Asia, and low-lying island nations.

This has become a major problem in UN climate negotiations. Developing nations from the global South have argued that most of the emissions reductions should be placed on the nations who caused the problem, so poorer nations can work to expand food production, health care, and electricity for their people. It's only fair that wealthier countries pay for cleaning up the climate mess that they're mostly responsible for, but some nationalist leaders used that as an out. When Donald Trump pulled the United States out of the Paris Agreement, an international treaty to combat climate change, he said, "The bottom line is that the Paris Accord is very unfair, at the highest level, to the United States." Trump targeted the Green Climate Fund, which would help poorer nations pay for a low-carbon transition, calling it a scheme to redistribute wealth from rich to poor countries.

Trump has openly denied the scientific consensus on climate change, claiming that it's a hoax made up by the Chinese. The fact is that more than eight million people die from air pollution every year, and many of these deaths are related to the burning of fossil fuels. And like those impacted by climate change, the people who experience the worst impacts of air pollution are low-income households and people of color.

Just north of where I live in Colorado, we see blatant examples of this kind of environmental racism. Extraction Oil and Gas has built a massive twenty-four-well frac pad less than one thousand feet from an elementary school playground in Greeley, Colorado. The wells were originally sited near a mostly white private school called Frontier Academy. When parents from Frontier protested, Extraction moved this industrial site next to Bella Romero Academy, a public school that's more than 80 percent Latinx. Extraction has gone ahead and fracked despite a lawsuit by the Sierra Club and the NAACP for environmental racism. Sadly, the injustice at Bella Romero is not an isolated example—it's part of a larger pattern.

Studies show that white people on average contribute to more air pollution in the United States than people of color but are less likely to feel its impacts. White people on average experience 17 percent less air pollution than they produce, while black and brown communities receive 61 percent more air pollution than their consumption habits create.

If you care about the environment, you have to pay attention to how connected our environment is to racial- and social-justice issues. Otherwise, you're not seeing the full picture.

People of color are far from the only group being impacted by the fossil fuel industry. Fracking is also invading many white suburban neighborhoods across the United States, and we're seeing lifelong Republicans enter the climate fight. Just fifty miles south of Greeley and Bella Romero are the communities of Broomfield and Thornton, where hundreds of wells are being sited near homes and schools. People of all party affiliations are fighting to keep out the fracking wells. Broomfield even had a Republican running for state representative who endorsed Proposition 112, a people's initiative to protect our communities from fracking that the oil and gas industry spent over $37 million to defeat.

Democrats often talk a better game than Republicans when it comes to climate change, but they are not immune to the power of money in politics and end up siding with the fossil fuel industry far too often. Take former Colorado Governor John Hickenlooper, a Democrat who has been beholden to fossil fuel companies since he worked at Buckhorn Petroleum. When five cities, including Broomfield, passed local bans on fracking, Hickenlooper's administration sued them all and overturned their restrictions. Thanks in part to his pro-fracking governorship, every Front Range county now has an *F* rating from the American Lung Association, and Denver now has the twelfth most polluted air in the country. That's the air my little brother and sister are breathing every day, and the expansion of this industry continues to push fracking closer to my home.

We see similar corporate influence in the Republican Party. There was a time when they were also talking about defeating climate change. Both George H. W. Bush and John McCain ran on it. But in 2004, Americans for Prosperity was founded by the Koch brothers as a political action committee (PAC). Right-wing billionaires simultaneously used this PAC to convince Republicans to vote against climate action with a "no climate tax" pledge and funded climate-denial propaganda. The scheme worked, and now most Republicans won't touch climate change.

The truth is that climate change is not a partisan

issue. A superstorm doesn't ask your political affiliation before wiping away your home. All these imaginary borders exist in order to disempower us, and they keep our movements fragmented and divided. And it's going to take us dropping these artificial barriers of partisan politics to really get down to solutions.

Throughout my involvement in the climate justice movement, one of the largest obstacles has been the world's failure to recognize climate change as a human issue. In the footsteps of my ancestors, part of my work is to honor the intrinsic connection between humans and our planet. The world has been at war with this ideology (and the people who live by it) for hundreds of years. The whole idea that the environment and climate are something outside of or separate from us came from an imperial European view of the world. Part of our journey as people who have suffered from colonization is rejecting this "power over nature" mentality. For myself and many indigenous communities, our need to protect the earth is a means of cultural survival.

As colonization spread around the world, it created and emphasized the barriers of national borders, class, race, religion, and political affiliation. But one of the most damaging colonial legacies from a climate perspective is the illusion that we are separate from our environment. This has created the greatest cultural disassociation with the climate crisis. Mainstream culture has presented the effects of climate change as something that only impacts systems of nature, and as a result, we've mentally removed ourselves from the conversation.

But climate change is quickly dismantling these illusionary boundaries and borders we've placed around it. Everything changes when the places we love are threatened. In 2013, the reality of what we're facing came home to the foothills of the Rocky Mountains. Colorado's most damaging flood and wildfire on record arrived just a few months apart. Once again, climate change went from an abstract, distant issue I cared about to something deeply personal that destroyed the mountains I grew up wandering and the homes of some of my closest friends.

If we wait for the floodwater to reach our doorstep, it will be too late.

From the coast to bustling cities to rural farm communities, our existence is inseparable from our environment. The progress we make must be anchored in the wisdom of our ancestors, who taught us that honoring our connection to the earth is the most sacred gift of all.

Yes this is critical, this is my resistance
Artists hold more power than these
crooked politicians . . .

Whether we care to admit it or not, our society is heavily based on an economic model that is built on the exploitation of human and natural resources. The linear idea of wealth in our society has fooled us into thinking that we have only two choices: a healthy planet or a thriving economy. The illusion that human systems are separate from what happens to the earth has made politicians, corporations, and individuals view our planet as an afterthought. This is clearly reflected in the platforms politicians run on every year, where climate change is left on the back burner. It's amazing to me that the "affordability" of ensuring a stable climate system is the main barrier for many people and politicians.

If we don't address this crisis now, the economic impacts could be more dire than anything we've seen in the last two hundred years. In fact, economists estimate that the impact from climate change by the end of the century is likely to be at least ten times as bad as the 2008 Great Recession. And this kind of economic disaster will not go away in a few years. It could last for generations.

In a society so reliant on an unbalanced economic model, what does it mean for our communities when the economy tanks? According to the World Bank,[1] it means an additional one hundred million people will be dragged into extreme poverty worldwide. Just to zoom in on agriculture, which employs over a billion people around the world: Our farms are gonna be screwed for a whooole bunch of reasons—everything from rising sea levels contaminating the soil with salt to extreme weather wrecking arable land. Millions of people will lose their jobs and their land, which is gonna hurt everyone, not just farmers.

1. The World Bank is an international organization that gives developmental assistance to middle-income and low-income countries.

Climate solutions need to take economic justice into account because if we perpetuate the same old top-down systems, we won't be able to solve our crisis holistically.

One idea that's taken the United States by storm is the Green New Deal, proposed by Congresswoman Alexandria Ocasio-Cortez and Senator Ed Markey. It's estimated that this initiative would create eighteen million jobs nationally and get us off fossil fuels in just over a decade. The front-end costs of the GND are perhaps the most important investment those in power will ever make. Think of it like this: Imagine your car's brakes are run-down. You know you probably need to fix them, but you don't want to spend the money. One day, you're going down a hill, and the brakes inevitably fail, and you crash into someone's house, causing hundreds of thousands of dollars' worth of damage. If we skimp on the problem now, we're going to have to pay a lot more later.

Currently, the US government is spending $649 billion annually to subsidize fossil fuels, more than ten times the budget for education. Redirecting the money the government is pouring into propping up the fossil fuel industry would more than finance the entire Just Transition of our energy economy. In the United States alone, this transition to 100 percent wind, water, and solar energy would save an additional $600 billion a year on health care costs from cleaner air and water and save an estimated forty-five thousand lives annually. The same move to 100 percent renewables in China would save over $6 trillion a year in health care costs and save more than six hundred thousand lives annually. The Solutions Project[2] has actually mapped out how every state and nearly every country could get to 100 percent renewables with a mix of solar, wind, hydro, tidal, wave, and geothermal energy.

While we can see that a Just Transition is possible, we need to make sure the way it's done doesn't follow the same colonial mindset that got us into this mess. People of color and low-income communities must have equity in the transition, with meaningful employment and community power. We can't afford

2. https://thesolutionsproject.org/why-clean-energy/#/map/countries/

another hierarchical energy model that exploits marginalized communities and increases racial and economic disparity. This mindset shift is also needed for workers in the fossil fuel industry, so they can be trained for good jobs in the new energy economy.

As we rebuild our communities in a way that sustains life, we have an opportunity to build a more just society. In the book *The Green Collar Economy*, Van Jones outlines the way this transition wouldn't just be beneficial for our environment but, if done correctly, would revitalize conditions for inner-city communities. Stepping into the future of our economies in the right way means less poverty, fewer people in prison, less air pollution, and a better future for America's poorest neighborhoods. But if the transition is run entirely by Silicon Valley and big energy businesses, the people that need this the most will be the last to receive its benefits.

This is much bigger than simply transitioning energy systems to save the planet. What needs to shift is our extraction-based economy that is unjust at its foundation. Through us reimagining our economies, we can build more resilient communities, create millions of clean jobs, save a lot of lives and money (both good things), and implement a financial system that balances the health of the people, the planet, and dat cash moneyyyy. We just gotta be quick enough to implement it before this whole ship crashes. Time is money, and we're running out fast.

This is Boombox Warfare
Gather in the cypher
Music draws the intersections,
    make the circles wider
Cool the earth's climate when
    I'm spitting fire . . .

When I was seven, my mom brought home a baby grand piano that she'd gotten from the Salvation Army. My godmother's friend was a renowned concert pianist who agreed to give me lessons for free. She started coming to my house every week and teaching me the basics of reading notes and time signatures, and how to count measures, but honestly, I didn't really care about all that. Instead of practicing the finger exercises and reading what she'd assigned, I started improvising, learning melodies by ear, and writing pieces I thought sounded good. When she came back, I asked her to help me write my own songs instead of learning other people's. For me, appreciating and understanding music came from a deep desire to create my own.

I was eight when I got my first hip-hop record. It was a burned CD of Michael Franti & Spearhead's album *Stay Human*. When I heard the first song on the album, "Oh My God," it instantly became my favorite song, and probably held number one until, like, 2015. The energy and soulful rhythm, the beautiful guitar melody, and the spacious, poetic vocals were mesmerizing. It was the first time I ever really sat down and listened to anybody rap. I was blown away by how the depth and lyricism balanced such a funky creative sound.

The whole record was mad political but maintained the sonic vibe to still make you dance. I hadn't heard anyone talk about revolution like this before. From Franti, I started listening to artists like Talib Kweli, KRS-One, and Flobots. Listening to Kweli's "Ballad of the Black Gold" and to Flobots's whole *Fight with Tools* album helped me understand how hip-hop is used as a tool to challenge oppressive systems and give voice to our communities.

In studying the history of how hip-hop culture began in the Bronx in the late '70s, it was clear to me that this ran much deeper than just entertainment. Hip-hop became a language for marginalized communities that were neglected, oppressed, and unheard, to reclaim their voices and tell the stories of the people.

This energy, this culture—it came into my life right when I needed it most.

I started speaking at climate events around the United States when I was pretty young, and I landed in the media over and over again because, for a lot of people, it was unusual to see someone my age out there on the front lines. When I turned nine, I started the third generation of Earth Guardians. We grew our youth crew, worked to ban pesticides in our city parks, and spoke out about the dangers of coal ash to protect our waterway systems. We worked to get bans and moratoriums on fracking. That was the beginning of the Earth Guardian Youth movement, which is now in over sixty countries. These actions led to even more media attention, and at age twelve, I had the opportunity to speak at the 2012 United Nations Conference on Sustainable Development

(Rio+20) in Brazil. It seemed like every weekend there was a protest I would speak at or an action that I was involved in.

Flash forward to the end of 2015: one of the most confusing times of my life. I'd taken a semester off from high school and was traveling all the time, either to speak about climate change or perform with my little bro, Itzcuauhtl. After nine years of constant movement, I felt like I was running on empty. The fire and passion that set me off at six years old seemed to have disappeared, along with my childhood. I found myself questioning everything about my path, my purpose, and my identity. As I watch my sixteen-year-old little brother now go through similar things to what I did, I'm reminded that an apathetic, rebellious mind state is something a lot of young people experience. It's that awkward stage between childhood and adulthood, when you're just starting to grow up. When I was his age, I began to feel that the path I was on was no longer fulfilling. The disconnect and indifference that I saw in so many of my peers was taking over how I saw the world.

At the time, I didn't know how to deal with depression or to tell people how I felt. The moment that shifted it all was when I started blending my activism with my music. I got to say everything I felt, everything I didn't understand, everything I'd never had the chance to say onstage or in the countless interviews I'd given. I began to tell my own story. Through my music, I reestablished a connection to my position as a leader in these movements. I came to life again.

It felt like, for the first fifteen years of my life, all these adults and journalists and followers had been crafting the narrative of who I was through their expectations and perceptions of me. Putting a pen in my hand gave me the power to redefine my story from a place of deep vulnerability and truth.

In 2018, I put out "Blu Ink," and it was the first time I'd released a song reflecting this new understanding of self. It felt like I'd let go of a huge weight. Then I put out a whole album about it called *Break Free*, which reflected the part of my life the rest of the world had tried to write for me, but in my own words, over beats

I'd written in my basement with my best friends. It was the most authentic expression of creativity and resistance for me. I went to LA and spent the better part of two years in a one-bedroom house in Culver City, working twelve hours a day with a brilliant, spiritual mixing wizard named Brian Hardin; Richard Vagner, a Russian violinist; and my barefoot Australian homie, Jaiia, to create an album that I needed to write. Not to make hits or write club bangers, but to reclaim my voice.

When I began to play these songs in venues for thousands of people all over the country, I saw that there is a generation of youth who need art like this. We're telling stories of our movements in a way people can meaningfully connect to.

I learned about the medicine in our music from my homie Nahko. The painful and wild journey of healing and change he reflected in his lyrics spoke to people so deeply. I saw it in the eyes of the people at his shows. People in tears, crying out in solidarity and celebration of the truths they found in his lyrics. I don't think I've ever seen an artist touch people the way Nahko does. When I began to see the same reaction in people watching my set, it showed me just how powerful this work is.

In the spring of 2018, my closest friends and I embarked on our first-ever tour together. After almost two years of working together on *Break Free*, we finally had the chance to share it with the world. The tour started in Burlington, Vermont, and ended with three shows in Florida. Every night we were in a different city, driving through towns and wilderness I'd never seen before. When I got onstage, it was about more than a performance. I got the chance to create an energy through my lyrics, the songs, the stories we told, and the movements and people I represented.

While statistics and science aim to change minds, art has always changed hearts. Every show was a challenge to strike a balance between having a strong message and having a compelling artistic presence. It's the trick I've spent the last few years learning. If all you have is a message, and the art isn't compelling on its own, the reach is limited. Creating music that has a vibe and also seamlessly weaves in your message—

that's when you begin to break down the barriers between movements and mainstream culture.

In 2019, I went to Frankfurt, Germany, with my DJ, mentor, and vegan culinary expert DJ Cavem, aka Chef Ietef, aka the plant-based trap king. I went to receive an award from the Senckenberg Museum for the work I'd done on climate change, and adding the lens of hip-hop turned the whole trip into a party. The day before the award ceremony, my DJ and I were set to give a talk to students from a bunch of different high schools about the work I was doing with the global organization the Earth Guardians. There were other speakers and activities, including a workshop on community organizing and a talk from one of my longtime heroes, environmentalist Felix Finkbeiner, who has been working to plant a trillion trees worldwide since he was nine years old. We closed the event with a performance, and since there was no stage, we pushed two tables together to rock a few songs. We ended up playing the fattest trap beats off my album *XI:XI* and started a mosh pit in the museum with a bunch of German high-school students. It was a fucking moment. The whole room was buzzing and celebrating our movement.

Bringing art into a space like that changes everything. At the beginning, the crowd was quiet and a little disengaged, and by the end, we were all jumping, moshing, and singing together. The next night at the fancy award ceremony, I had all the wealthy German investors and financial supporters of the museum out of their seats and clapping while I rapped my acceptance speech. Two days later, at, like, 7:00 p.m. on a Monday (with no alcohol, mind you), we threw a hip-hop party in the back of the Lululemon outlet in Frankfurt and had about three hundred people pull up to the show to get down. A few of the organizers from the local FridaysForFuture climate march came, and the whole night was about celebration and building community. The stories and ideas of our work were woven through the whole event, but not in a way that felt stuffy, preachy, and political. We brought a completely different energy to the conversation.

The story we've been telling about climate change

has failed to truly evoke and inspire connection because it has lacked imagination and creativity. You won't believe the amount of times I've gone to events with the exact same audience, saying the exact same thing about sustainability or the environment and not gotten anywhere. Even people who care and mean well have been operating within this fixed box of "activism." This stereotype has kept so many people away from being a part of these movements.

When Al Gore first started talking about climate change, a lot of people thought this whole thing was about hippies and climate scientists trying to save polar bears. So much of the environmental discussion has been about really specific existential issues that seem far away, like ice caps melting and parts per million of carbon dioxide in the atmosphere. It requires a certain amount of privilege to be able to put energy toward that. If someone is living in government-assisted housing in a low-income neighborhood with parents working full-time, it can be hard to view things through the lens that many environmentalists have offered.

We succeed in contributing the most to the world when it comes from a place of authentic passion. I've seen this firsthand by experiencing how hip-hop can redirect and inspire people.

Art can build a bridge to fill those gaps of connection. With so many titles, identities, and differences that often separate us, music's power to bring us together and humanize our stories is what makes it such a crucial piece of how we are going to define our movements going forward.

The anthems that propel our movements further, the iconic visuals that stick in our head, the art that paints a picture of what we're fighting for—these things bring life to our fight, and considering what we're up against, we need a whole lot of that right now.

*I can feel the sound reaching through
   the speakers
Rhythm of the movement
Revolution through the tweeters
Lift a generation up, move the masses
   when the bass hits
Imma touch the world with what started
   in the basement . . .*

—Xiuhtezcatl Martinez

In 1992, in Haleakala Crater on the island of Maui, Hawaii, my mama, Tamara Roske, had a vision of young people standing together across the globe to protect their future. She dreamed of millions of youth gathered at sacred sites and landmarks all over the world, demanding change. This vision manifested into an accredited high school with sixty students and nine teachers that following year. Every single class was dedicated to connecting youth to their voice and passion by leveraging a new education model to create change. They named the school "The Earth Guardian School."

The Earth Guardians have been involved in many huge wins in protecting and revitalizing their community. I've heard stories from my older siblings, who were students at the school, and I've seen old, laminated articles from the '90s that laid out the amazing work they'd done, such as banning junk mail in the post offices, planting thousands of sandalwood trees, and performing at dozens of events across the Hawaiian Islands.

In 1995, the Dalai Lama gifted the school with the Children's Torch of Hope, which set off a twenty-nine-state tour across the United States. The Earth Guardians performed, spoke, and rallied at dozens of schools, communities, and conferences across the nation. Every event began with a ceremonial lighting of this torch. (And the youth ambassador from Mexico in charge of that ceremony also just happened to be my dad.) With my grandpa driving the huge school bus city to city, the vision of putting power back in the hands of the youth was waking up people in every community. Some folks were so charged up that they would hop on the bus for days at a time to join different legs of the tour before going back home.

Almost twenty-five years later, the vision of Earth

Guardians has grown into a global community, embodying the dream my mom had all those years ago. Earth Guardians has hundreds of active crews on the ground in over fifty-five countries worldwide. We are working to build resilience and diversity into our movements by putting creative youth at the forefront of designing and implementing the solutions our world needs. EG supports a thriving network of youth leaders worldwide, has implemented climate leadership curricula into twenty thousand classrooms across the United States, and launched Earth Tracks, an app that acts like a Fitbit for the planet and helps us take action in reducing our environmental footprint. We're working every day to strengthen our generation's platform to create our own future.

Earth Guardians' work is more necessary and urgent than ever, as the youth of the world are continuing to rise to power and shape our culture. From Black Lives Matter to the LGBTQIA+ movement to FridaysForFuture and the March for Our Lives, we are flooding the scene and showing the world that we are not willing to quietly wait for change to be made on our behalf.

I think that one of the biggest differences between our generation and our parents' is that we understand the power of building intersectional movements. The urgency of our climate crisis, paired with the fearless leadership of our generation, is creating a new standard for how we need to view this issue. I'd say that almost anyone working on climate now, even my older, white homies like Paul Hawken and Bill McKibben, knows that we need a diverse movement with voices that represent the true breadth of the issues we face. Our generation is tearing down the walls that have divided us.

From Mauna Kea to Flint, Michigan, to the front lines of nearly every major environmental action, we're reminding the world that indigenous people and marginalized communities need to be at the forefront of this fight.

As our ability to communicate has gotten easier, the lines that have separated us are fading. Across industries, countries, religions, professions, and academic paths, people are really starting to get it. We're acknowledging that struggles for justice—

whether they be environmental, social, political, or racial—are intrinsically linked, and so are the solutions to these crises. Our neighborhoods, our communities, and our homes are just as much a part of our environment as the oceans, forests, and mountains.

So where do you fit into all this? The misconception that activism has to look and feel a certain way is dying out as our generation is rejecting the limitations placed on us and seeing the bigger picture. Maybe you see yourself as an architect who will build more energy-efficient homes. Maybe you see yourself as a farmer growing local, delicious, organic food for your community. Maybe you see yourself as an artist who will help expand people's consciousness.

Being a part of these movements begins where you're inspired to plug in. Just in the last few years, I've seen support coming from the most random places. And it's blown me away. From seeing pro boxer Mikey Garcia cosign the Earth Guardians movement, to collaborating with Jaden Smith, to getting requests to add an installation about the movement in one of the biggest museums in Vietnam, I've seen more diverse tactics and approaches than ever before. Billions of years of evolution have created the perfect conditions for humans to exist, and in the same way that we've disrupted that sacred balance, we have the power as a global community to restore it—to create more prosperity and justice than ever before. I believe the climate crisis can inspire the best in humanity. It is challenging us to be our most creative, resilient, visionary selves.

We can protect our communities from climate disaster without being swept away by fear. We can enjoy all this planet has to offer while ensuring that future generations will have the same opportunities. We can challenge everything broken about our world while keeping our focus on the solutions we want to build.

It's on us, on you, to reclaim your power, to play your part in one of the most significant moments in history. Scientists project that we have a decade to reduce the greatest impacts of our climate crisis. These are about to be the wildest ten years of our lives. I believe in our generation's power to rise to the challenge, meet this deadline, and change history. Taking that first step, no matter how small, is up to you.

Are you in?

ABOUT US

Pocket Change Collective was born out of a need for space. Space to think. Space to connect. Space to be yourself. And this is your invitation to join us.

These books are small, but they are mighty. They ask big questions and propose even bigger solutions. They show us that no matter where we come from or where we're going, we can all take part in changing the communities around us. Because the possibilities of how we can use our space for good are endless.

So thank you. Thank you for picking this book up. Thank you for reading. Thank you for being a part of the Pocket Change Collective.